# FINGER GUITAR STYLE

# Jazz Standards

**Arranged by
JAMIE FINDLAY**

T0042557

This publication is not for sale in
the EU and/or Australia
or New Zealand.

Cover guitar courtesy of Crown Music, Milwaukee, Wisconsin

ISBN 978-0-7935-6567-2

HAL•LEONARD®
CORPORATION
7777 W. BLUEMOUND RD. P.O. BOX 13819 MILWAUKEE, WI 53213

Visit Hal Leonard Online at
**www.halleonard.com**

# Jazz Standards

# All the Things You Are

Lyrics by Oscar Hammerstein II
Music by Jerome Kern

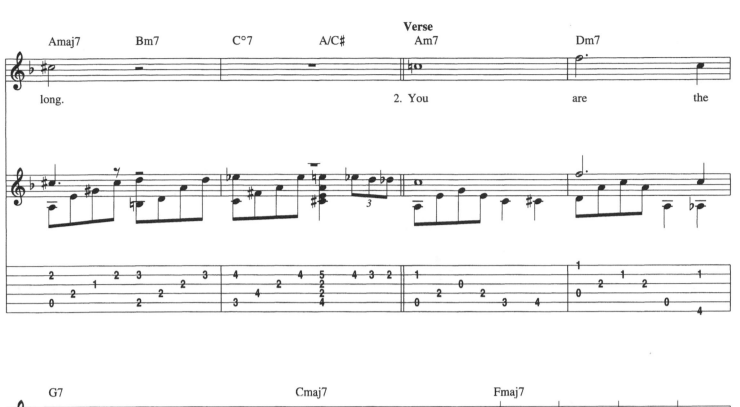

long.  2. You are the

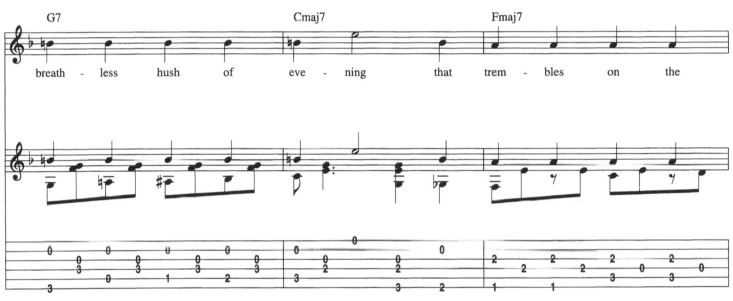

breath - less hush of eve - ning that trem - bles on the

brink of a love - ly song. You are the

an - gel glow that lights a star. _____

_____ The dear - est things I know _____ are what you

are. _____ 3. Some - day my

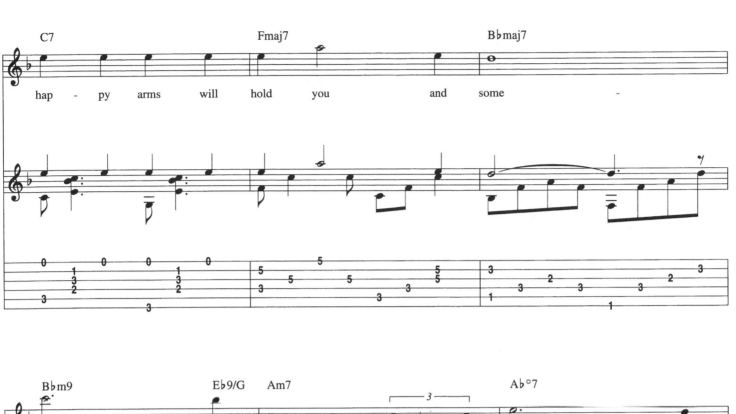

hap - py arms will hold you and some -

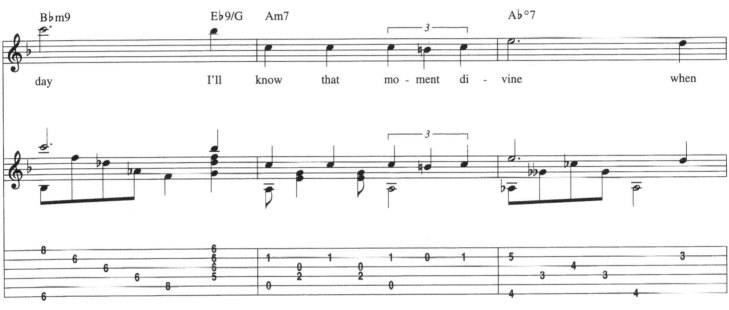

day I'll know that mo - ment di - vine when

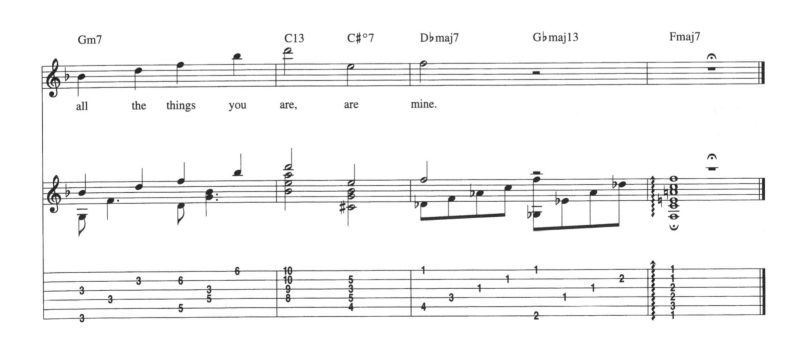

all the things you are, are mine.

# Autumn Leaves
## (Les Feuilles Mortes)

English lyric by Johnny Mercer
French lyric by Jacques Prevert
Music by Joseph Kosma

old win - ter's song. But I miss you most of

all, my dar - ling, when

au - tumn leaves start to fall.

# Black Orpheus

**By Louiz Bonfa**

# Bluesette

**Words by Norman Gimbel**
**Music by Jean Thielemans**

find a some - one to be true to.

Two lov - ing arms he can nest - le in and

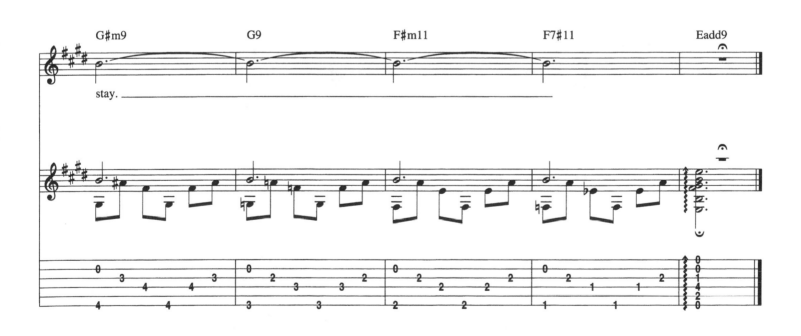

stay. _____

# Body and Soul

**Words by Edward Heyman, Robert Sour and Frank Eyton**
**Music by John Green**

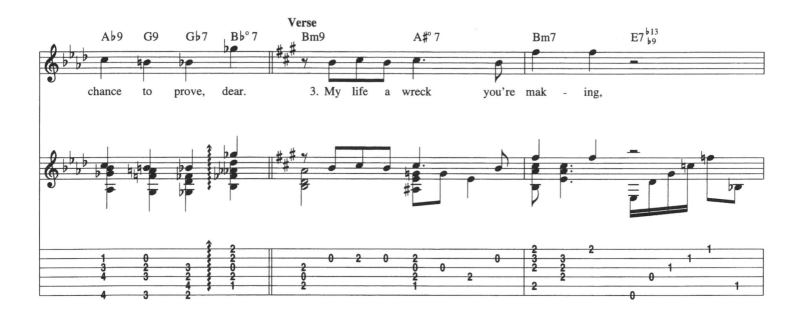

chance to prove, dear.   3. My life a wreck you're mak - ing,

you know I'm yours   for just the tak - ing.   I'd glad - ly sur -

ren - der   my - self to you,   body and soul.

# Fly Me to the Moon (In Other Words)

**Words and Music by Bart Howard**

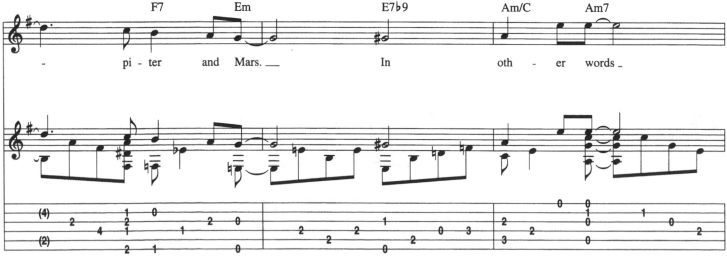

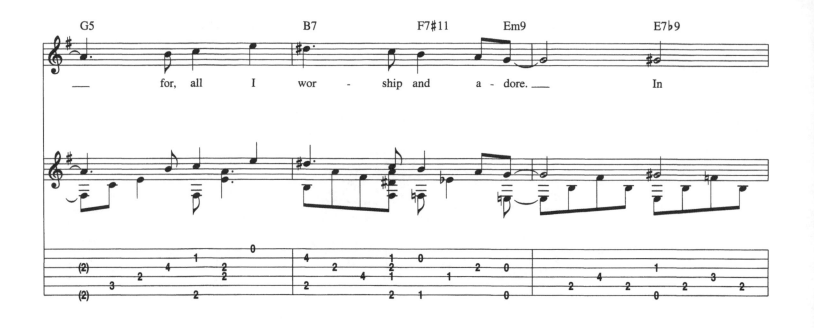

for, all I wor - ship and a - dore. __ In

oth - er words, __ please be true, in

oth - er words, I love you! __

# Have You Met Miss Jones?

**Words by Lorenz Hart**
**Music by Richard Rodgers**

un - der - stands     I'm     a     man     who     must          be     free."

**Bridge**

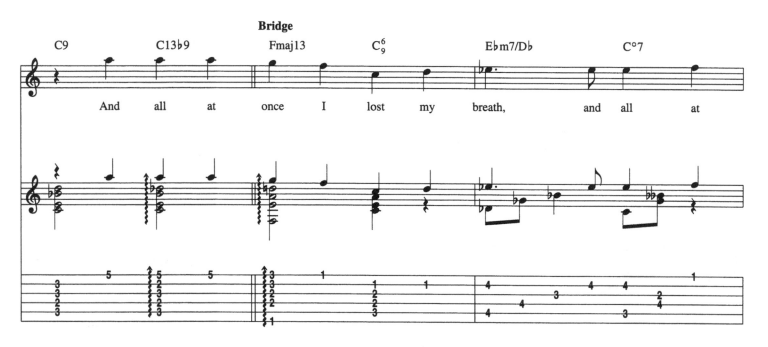

And     all     at     once     I     lost     my     breath,          and     all     at

once     was     scared     to     death,     and     all     at     once     I     owned     the

# The Girl from Ipanema
## (Garôta de Ipanema)

**English Words by Norman Gimbel**
**Original Words by Vinicius de Moraes**
**Music by Antonio Carlos Jobim**

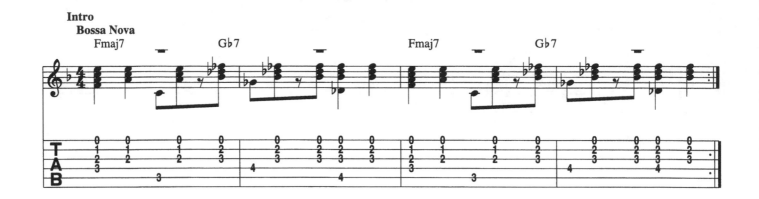

1.Tall and tan and young ___ and love - ly the girl ___ from I - pa - ne -
2. *See Additional Lyrics*

- ma goes walk - ing and when ___ she pas - ses, each one ___ she pas - ses goes,

from Ip - a - ne - ma goes walk - in' and when she pas - ses I smile

but she does-n't see _____ she just does-n't see

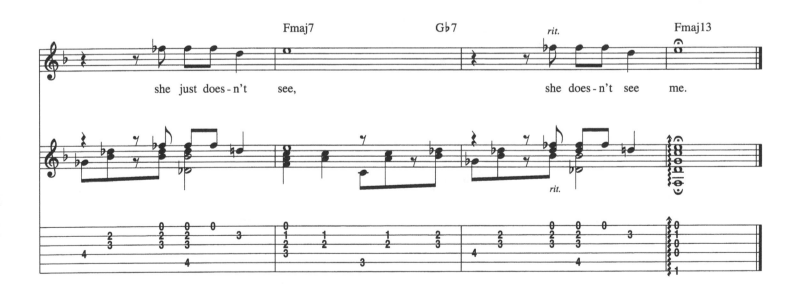

she just does-n't see, she does-n't see me.

*Additional Lyrics*

2. When she walks it's like a samba
That swings so smoothe and swags so gentle that
When she passes, each one she passes goes, "Ahh."

# God Bless' the Child

**Words and Music by Arthur Herzog Jr. and Billie Holiday**

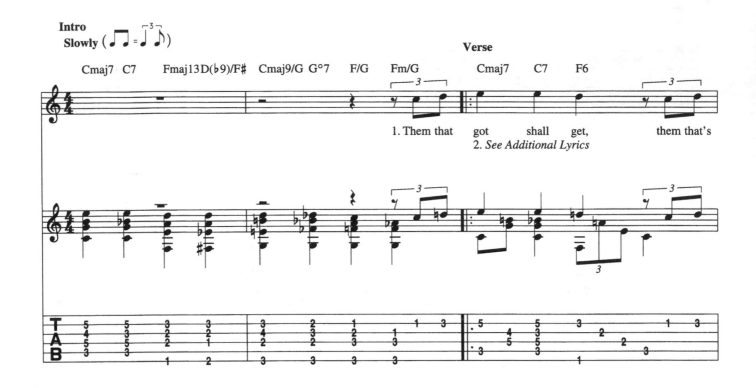

crowd - in' 'round the door.        When you're gone and

spend - in' end,        they        don't        come        no

**Verse**

more.        3. Rich re - la - tions give        crust of bread,        and such.        You can

*Additional Lyrics*

Yes, the strong gets more, while the weak ones fade,
Empty pockets don't ever make the grade;
Mama may have, Papa may have,
But God bless' the child that's got his own!
That's got his own.

# How High the Moon

**Words by Nancy Hamilton**
**Music by Morgan Lewis**

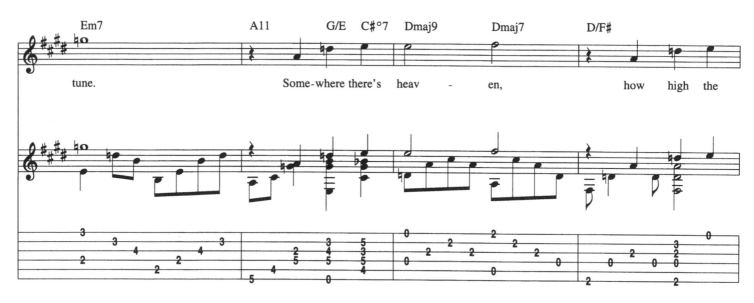

*Additional Lyrics*

2. Somewhere there's music,
   It's where you are.
   Somewhere there's heaven,
   How near how far.
   The darkest night would shine
   If you would come to me soon...

# How Insensitive

## (Insensatez)

**Original Words by Vinicius de Moraes**
**English Words by Norman Gimbel**
**Music by Antonio Carlos Jobim**

MCA music publishing

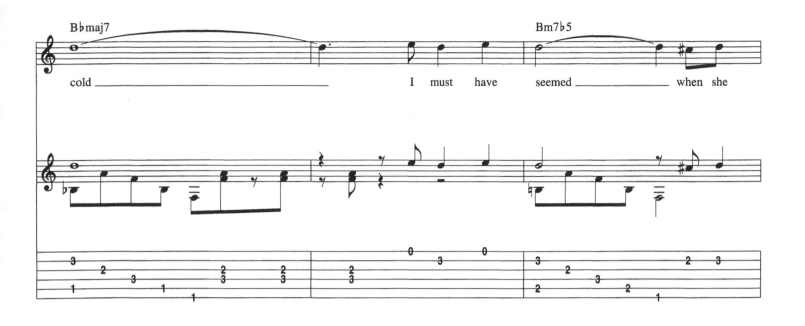

cold _____ I must have seemed _____ when she

told me so sin - cere - ly. _____

**Chorus**

Why _____ she must have asked _____ did I just

# I've Grown Accustomed to Her Face

**Words by Alan Jay Lerner**
**Music by Frederick Loewe**

1. I've grown ac-cus-tomed to her face, she al-most
2. *See Additional Lyrics*

makes the day be-gin. I've grown ac-cus-tomed to the tune she

whist-les night and noon. Her smiles, her frowns, her

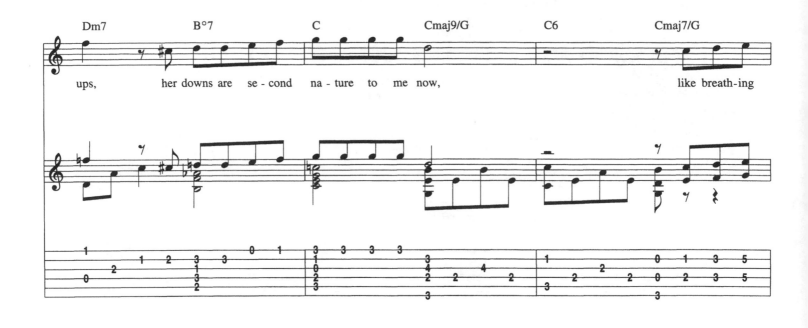

ups,        her downs are se - cond    na - ture   to   me   now,                                                    like breath-ing

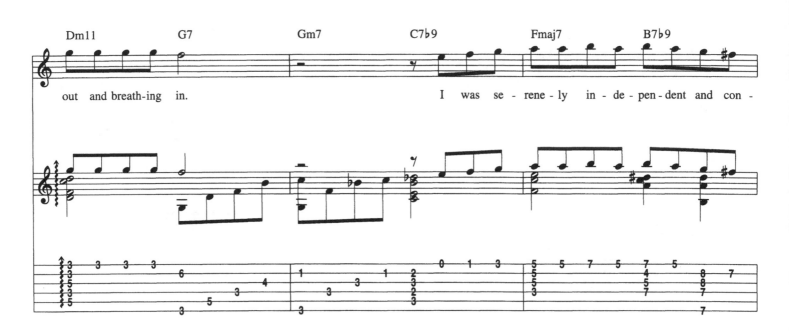

out  and breath-ing   in.                                        I   was  se - rene - ly   in - de - pen - dent and con -

tent   be - fore   we   met;                                        sure - ly    I    could    al - ways    be    that

*Additional Lyrics*

2. I've grown accustomed to her face.
   She almost makes the day begin.
   I've gotten used to hear her say, "Good morning."
   Everyday, her joys, her woes, her lows
   Are second nature to me now,
   Like breathing out and breathing in.
   I'm very grateful she's a woman
   And so easy to forget.
   Rather like a habit one can always break and yet
   I've grown accustomed to the trace of
   Something in the air,
   Accustomed to her face.

# Lover Man (Oh, Where Can You Be?)

By Jimmy Davis, Roger "Ram" Ramirez and Jimmy Sherman

MCA music publishing

**Bridge**

*Additional Lyrics*

2. The night is cold, and I'm so all alone.
   I'd give my soul just to call you my own.
   Got a moon above me, but no one to love me;
   Lover man, oh where can you be?

3. Someday we'll meet and you'll dry all my tears,
   Then whisper sweet little things in my ears.
   Huggin' and a-kissin', oh, what we've been missin';
   Lover man, oh where can you be?

# My Funny Valentine

**Words by Lorenz Hart**
**Music by Richard Rodgers**

**Verse**

Dm7♭5     G7♭13 B°7    Cm7     Cm9     B°7     Cm7/B♭

3. Don't change a hair for me, not if you

F9/A    F13    A♭maj7   Gm11    Dm7♭5   G7♭9    Cm7    B13

care for me. Stay lit - tle Val - en - tine stay.

B♭m7    A7♭5    A♭maj7   Gm7    Fm9    B♭7    E♭6

Each day is Val - en-tine's Day.

# My Romance

**Words by Lorenz Hart**
**Music by Richard Rodgers**

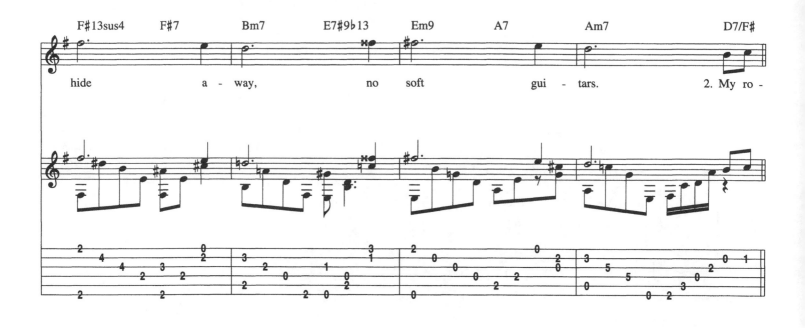

hide a - way, no soft gui - tars. 2. My ro -

**Verse**

mance does-n't need a cas - tle ris - ing in Spain, nor a

dance to a con - stant-ly sur - pris - ing re - frain. Wide a -

wake, I can make my most fan - tas - tic dreams come

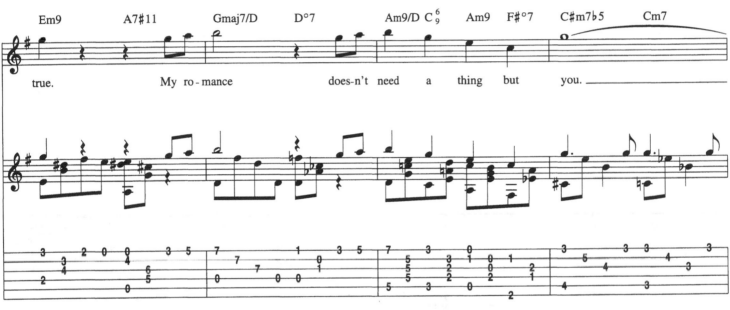

true. My ro - mance does-n't need a thing but you. ___

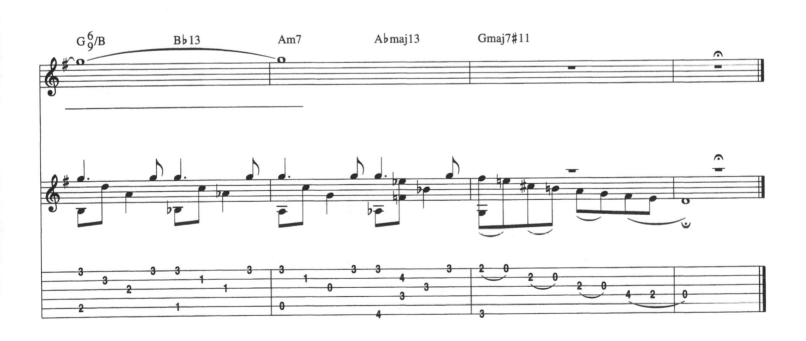

# Satin Doll

**Words by Johnny Mercer and Billy Strayhorn**
**Music by Duke Ellington**

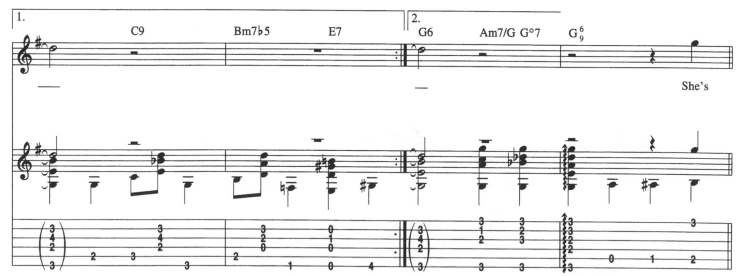

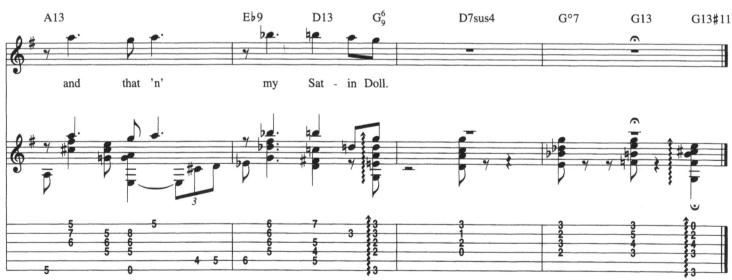

*Additional Lyrics*

2. Baby, shall we go out skippin'?
Careful, amigo, you're flippin'.
Speaks Latin, my Satin Doll.

# Stella by Starlight

**Words by Ned Washington**
**Music by Victor Young**

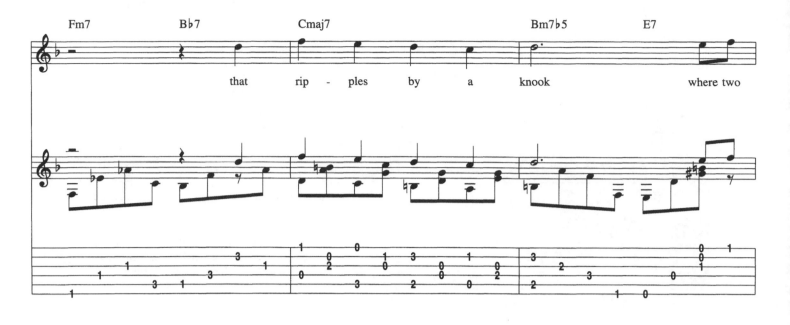

that rip - ples by a knook where two

lov - ers hide. That great sym - phon - ic

theme; _____ that's Stel - la by Star - light

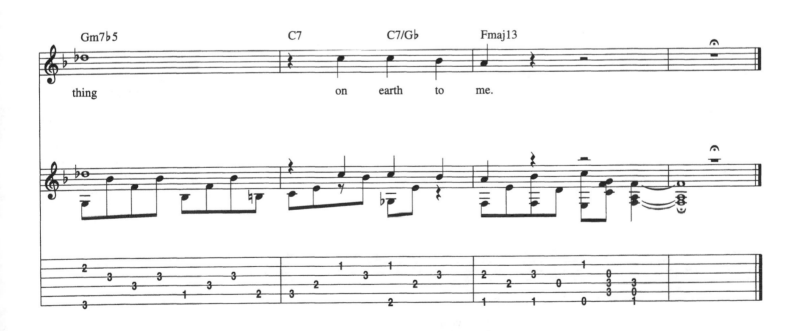

# Speak Low

**Words by Ogden Nash**
**Music by Kurt Weill**

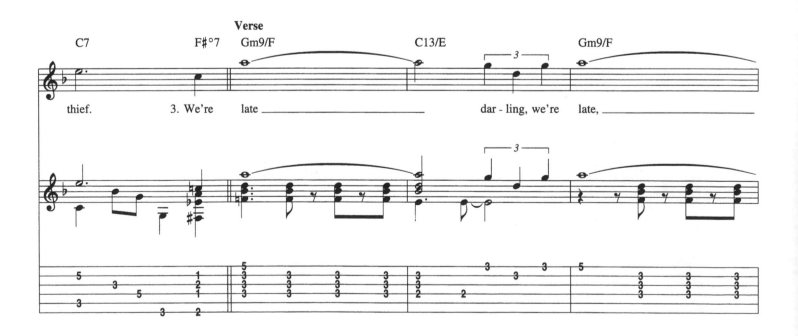

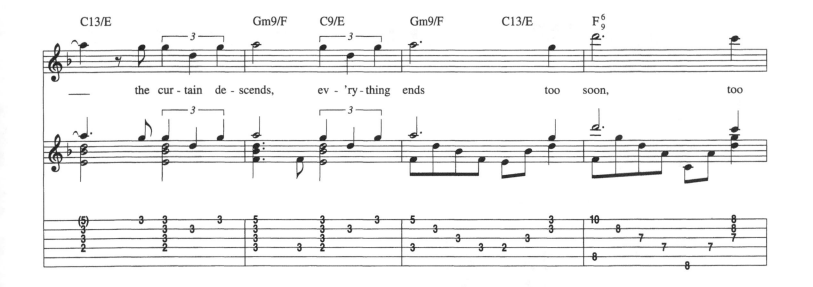

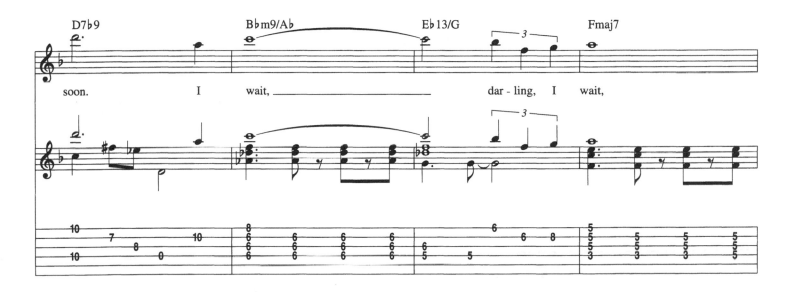

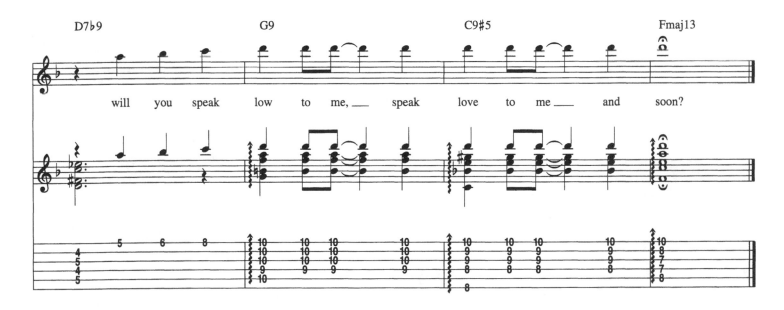

*Additional Lyrics*

2. Speak low, darling, speak low,
   Love is a spark lost in the dark
   Too soon, too soon, I feel....

# There Will Never Be Another You

Lyric by Mack Gordon
Music by Harry Warren

***Additional Lyrics***

2. There will be other lips that I may kiss,
   But they won't thrill me like yours used to do.
   Yes, I may dream a million dreams, but how can they come true
   If there will never, ever be another you?

# Stompin' at the Savoy

**Words and Music by Benny Goodman, Edgar Sampson, Chick Webb and Andy Razaf**

*Additional Lyrics*

2. Your form, just like a clingin' vine.
Your lips, so warm and sweet as wine.
Your cheek, so soft and close to mine,
Divine!